Snow Globe Days
Change Can Be an Adventure

By Kathleen Stefancin

Illustrations by Sherri Marteney

For more information visit: www.smartpicks.com

ISBN #978-0-9764785-5-3

Book design, layout and illustrations by Sherri Marteney

Dedications

Kathleen- To my parents who taught me to look for God's goodness in life's little challenges and to always be kind.

Kylea - Thank you to my family who has been a source of stability no matter what life transitions I have encountered.

I remember the shaking of my snow globe one day.
I was lost in the flurry and could not find my way.

Bouncing and tumbling uncontrollably around
until I suddenly landed upside down.

Wandering in a land not so very well-known,
I was scared to be in that place all on my own.

Change can be a challenge for a girl like me,
who likes things the same to a certain degree.

The things I once treasured had all been in place.
I had a life I enjoyed and loved to embrace.

Today's assignment:

pgs. 2-5

Every day had been neat and very much the same,
a consistent view I would again gladly claim.

But then, when you least expect it, everything can change,
and your whole world can suddenly become very strange.

So what do you do when you are all alone
in a place that feels scary and so unknown?

Were there new places to go or actions to take?
Perhaps there would be some new friends I could make.

There were things I did as I found my way.
It started the day I began to pray.

I finally let go of things I'd outgrown...
time for a new start with the faith I'd been shown.

My mom knew my struggle and what I'd been through.
She always stood by me in all that was new.

I reached out to hold onto her kind, helping hand.
She gave me the tools to navigate this new land.

So I pushed aside the snow in that old familiar space
and enjoyed the new adventures that were now in its place.

Change can be difficult for a girl like me,
who likes things the same to a certain degree.

I look in my heart for the answers I seek,
to find wisdom that says I'm distinctly unique.

As I accepted my struggle, I began to progress,
finding the gifts and talents that I wanted to express.

Whispers of the future seemed to call and say,
"There's so much goodness that is coming your way."

I was stronger than I know and much more than I think.
I see new opportunities between each tender blink.

As the snow settled, I stood firmly on the ground,
and began doing things that turned out quite profound.

Now I breathe a familiar breath of stability
as it brings to mind joyful gratitude and humility.

I am prepared for my next snow globe day.
With my new tools and talents, I won't lose my way.

Although change is difficult for a girl like me,
I've learned it can be an adventure.
I certainly agree!

Parents Pages

By Kylea Rorabaugh

Taking the First Steps of Change

Loss of life as it once was can include the loss of friends, pets, family members, a job, health, familiarity, celebration, travel, a new home, etc.

When you think about something changing, you might feel **SCARED**, or you might feel **EXCITED**.

If the change feels scary, what is one thing you can do to feel less scared?

EXAMPLE: If you move to a new town, find a playground you like. Think about the part of the playground that is usually your favorite. Maybe it's the slides. Try out all the new slides and decide which one is your favorite.

If you feel excited, what will keep you feeling excited?

EXAMPLE: If you go to a new school, think about one thing each day that you like about your new school, classmates, or teacher. Is there something you love about your new classroom? Who seems to be the friendliest? What's your favorite part about your new teacher?

Tools to Help with Change

Change is difficult, whether it is positive or negative. Anytime you experience change, consider the CHALLENGES it will present and the potential for GOODNESS it will bring.

Three-Step Process
If the change you are experiencing seems challenging, consider this three-step process:

1 **Allow yourself to process the pain the change may bring.**

EXAMPLE: Journal about all of the emotions that you feel or talk through your emotions with a trusted friend.

2 **Choose one way you can begin to accept the change today.**

EXAMPLE: Remind yourself throughout the day that although change can be hard, it is part of life. It is part of the way we grow, learn, and add spice to life.

3 **Consider one thing about the change that you are grateful for.**

EXAMPLE: Recognize that although you'll miss the way things were in your previous home, such as your beloved neighbors, there is beauty in the newness of your home now… perhaps the way the sun shines through the window of your new home or the beauty of the giant oak tree out back.

Reframing Tool

When faced with a challenge, **reframe** it!

Notice the troubling thought, feeling, or struggle rather than ignore it.

EXAMPLE OF A THOUGHT: There's no way I'll get everything done. I'm so overwhelmed.

Then, restate it in a way that creates hope, a positive action, or a thought that moves you forward (make sure it is believable).

EXAMPLE OF A REFRAME: Though I feel defeated and overwhelmed with my to-do's, I know I can accomplish them as long as I tackle one task at a time.

Practice.

Finding Your Purpose

What are some of your favorite things? What makes you feel so happy inside?

EXAMPLES: helping other people, drawing/coloring/creating something, playing tag, or hide-and-go-seek.

What are some things you are really good at?

EXAMPLES: art, sports, games, reading, science, or being kind to others.

How can you use the things you love and the things you are good at to make someone else smile or have a good day?

EXAMPLE: If you love to help other people and are really good at being a kind person, you might think about taking flowers to an elderly friend in a nursing home or sending a card to a family member who is sick.

About the Authors

Kathleen Stefancin is a registered dietitian, creative writer, photographer, and founder of Smart Picks, LLC. She has authored a series of award-winning nutritional stories for kids, including *The Fruit Flies Picnic*, *The Fish Who Wished He Could Eat Fruit*, and *Molly the Monkey Finds a Pineapple.* Her writing has expanded to include stories about emotional health and well-being. *Snow Globe Days* is the first in the new series. Kathleen holds a BA in dietetics and an MS in Nutrition. She resides in Ohio with her cat Callie and hopes to inspire young readers to live happy, healthy lifestyles.

Kylea Rorabaugh is in private practice specializing in Cognitive Behavior Therapy methods, offering tools and strategies that set her clients up for long-term success. She holds a BA in psychology and an MA in counseling. Kylea resides in Missouri with her husband of 23 years and her 2 teenage sons. She loves coffee, kitties, and savoring life with her family.

www.ingramcontent.com/pod-product-compliance
Lightning Source LLC
Chambersburg PA
CBHW042106040426
42448CB00002B/157